Accelerated Learning: Proven Advanced Strategies for Effective Memorization, Better Organization, and Unbreakable Concentration

By

Alex Medler

Copyright: Published in the United States by Alex Medler / ©
Alex Medler.

Text Copyright © Alex Medler

All rights reserved. No part of this guide may be reproduced in
any form without permission in writing from the publisher
except in the case of brief quotations embodied in critical
articles or reviews.

Legal & Disclaimer

The information contained in this book is not designed to
replace or take the place of any form of medicine or
professional medical advice. The information in this book has
been provided for educational and entertainment purposes
only.

The information contained in this book has been compiled
from sources deemed reliable, and it is accurate to the best of
the Author's knowledge; however, the Author cannot
guarantee its accuracy and validity and cannot be held liable
for any errors or omissions. Changes are periodically made to
this book. You must consult your doctor or get professional
medical advice before using any of the suggested remedies,
techniques, or information in this book.

Upon using the information contained in this book, you agree to hold harmless the Author from and against any damages, costs, and expenses, including any legal fees potentially resulting from the application of any of the information provided by this guide. This disclaimer applies to any damages or injury caused by the use and application, whether directly or indirectly, of any advice or information presented, whether for breach of contract, tort, negligence, personal injury, criminal intent, or under any other cause of action.

You agree to accept all risks of using the information presented inside this book. You need to consult a professional medical practitioner in order to ensure you are both able and healthy enough to participate in this program.

Table of Contents

Introduction

Accelerated learning is a modern teaching method introduced originally in 1976 and has, over the last 40 years, evolved from its humble beginnings as a unique concept into a universally accepted, although controversial, learning system.

In this e-book, I shall present the basics of Accelerated Learning and then delve deeper into the specific teaching methods that make up the whole system.

Accelerated learning is a constantly evolving system, and as more and more information is received from various sources, the base concepts advance and morph into new concepts. While this system is liberal, the original core does not change; just like the human skeleton, the muscles around it might grow and change, but the skeleton stays the same.

The chapters are arranged in a stepwise fashion; I present the history and concept of Accelerated Learning in the first chapter. The remaining chapters are dedicated to the specific core method used in the system, and I will finish with an unbiased conclusion.

What you will notice is that I do not include the use of technology as a main component. This is because technology is a tool, and while it has been instrumental in helping improve knowledge management, it is not a replacement for the human mind and, as such, must be placed alongside all other implements and accessories used to help us learn.

Technology has enabled us to step out of the conventional classroom, and it has given us a heightened approach to visual learning. It is one of the key supporting tools in accelerated learning but not the main one, as you will find out when reading this guide.

I hope that, once you read this book, you will accept the different approach that Accelerated Learning provides and incorporate some, if not all, the various methods into your daily life.

What is Accelerated Learning?

Accelerated Learning (AL) is a model of teaching and learning that goes beyond the current standard trends of teaching methods. The core of accelerated learning is to understand that the individual can experience learning from all five senses, as well as from social interactions. A comprehensive, holistic approach is the essential basis of this subject.

History

Accelerated learning has evolved since it was first introduced by the Bulgarian professor and psychotherapist, Dr. Georgi Lozanov, in Sophia in 1966, where Dr. Lozanov founded the Suggestology Research Institute. This grew into a movement that swept across the US, and in 1976, "suggestopedia" was renamed Accelerated Learning.

Suggestopedia stands for Suggestion and Pedagogy. Lozanov believed learning would be increased when it was a pleasurable and natural process, rather than a forced process. He integrated role-playing, art, music, and games as methods to accelerate understanding and comprehension of knowledge. Suggestopedia is all about the learning environment as much as it is about the content. His approach was in direct contrast to the mainstream Spartan environment approach, focusing students on a central "blackboard" and direct teaching model.

From Suggestopedia to Accelerated Learning

The name suggestopedia was dropped in the US; it changed to Accelerated Learning, which was much more "marketable" than the more comic "suggestopedia" name. It also represents the significant changes that the original suggestopedia model provided, with the continued research in learning methods, different bits of intelligence, psychology, and neuroscience.

The new Accelerated Learning technique, which is constantly evolving with continuous adaptation to new styles and methods, is completely separate in its core from other teaching methods. What this method presents at its core is the phenomena of suggestion and the way we express our desires, feelings, and hopes. Essentially, AL is about making the individual want to learn, to love the process of learning, and then, the individual will learn and a faster rate, even when using standard methods for obtaining knowledge.

The core of AL is that "attitude" is at the forefront of knowledge gaining. This means a very intelligent person will not gain knowledge properly if not stimulated to do so, while another person might gain great knowledge when presented with the right incentives and stimuli to accelerate the learning process.

What is Learning?

Learning is the ability to comprehend and understand the knowledge stored in memory. Learning is not intelligence; it is a process where we obtain information. Intelligence is the speed at which we can learn, and together, the two provide the ability to question knowledge and build theories and outcomes based on what has been learned and what is being learned. Memory is mandatory, so we can recall knowledge already learned and use it to help us advance core skills and understandings.

AL is a process that tries to make the learning stage not just easier, but more enjoyable. As such, the name Accelerated Learning is misleading, since AL does not speed up learning; it just facilitates the stimuli to help people enjoy learning and continue to learn more without being urged or pushed.

> ***Learning = Comprehension, Understanding, and Memory. Where Memory is the databank, comprehension is how we obtain the information, and understanding is how we process the information into knowledge. Intelligence is the speed at which our brain operates in manipulating all these activities together.***

One fundamental difference between AL and conventional teaching is that AL requires the administrator of learning to understand the basics of emotional intelligence. Emotional Intelligence (EQ) is how the individual understands their own emotions, and the emotions of others, and uses this understanding to control both themselves and the way others will act and react in any given situation. EQ is not about speed; it is about the perception of emotions and habits. Once a teacher becomes adept at EQ, it will be easier for them to apply AL.

The Accelerated Learning Framework

The Accelerated Learning framework is structured to meet and match every individual's abilities to learn, delivering them the exact incentives and conditions to learn. While the framework is structured, the system is constantly changing and adapting over time.

The AL framework is made up of seven core elements, as suggested by Howard Gardner in 1993. Gardner and others based these elements on the original theory and practice of suggestology. Since the 1970's, suggestology has been adopted by a number of researchers and authors, all of whom added to the original framework and developed the modern AL system.

<u>The seven core elements are:</u>

1. Verbal-linguistic. This is where words are arranged into meaning and order.
2. Musical. In which there is a sensitivity to pitch, melody, rhythm, and tone.
3. Mathematically logical. This implies logical order with reasoned patterns.
4. Spatial. This is how the individual views the world and recreates it based on perception.

5. Bodily-kinesthetic. This is how the body and its parts can be manipulated for sense and spatial awareness and touch.
6. Inter-personal. This is where social interaction comes to the fore, through group activities and articulating self to others and others with self.
7. Intra-personal. This is where the individual perceives themselves, looking into themselves, and understanding with respect to self.

In order to understand these seven cores, it is imperative to understand the six methods used in learning and apply the seven cores to each method effectively.

<u>These six methods are:</u>

1. Memory hooks: A memory hook is a method that links to pieces of information in a single sentence using a theme of words that appear to be logical. Memory hooks are used in PR and advertising and lead people to believe in absolute rubbish while sounding so perfectly true.
   For example, A Clean Home or Business Is a Happy Home. This might sound logical, but there is no real connection between clean homes and happiness. Another example: Achievement deserves recognition.

Why? Who says it does? But the sentence sounds sane, logical and even a must.

2. Multi-sensory Learning: This includes all the sensory methods.

    a. Visual: This is where all things visual are used to deliver information. It includes the concept of mind mapping, which is a sort of chunking method but specific to the visual learning process.

    b. Aural: Using music and sound to elicit learning responses.

    c. Verbal: Using speech to deliver information, this concept includes what is termed "call it out aloud." Here, you use the sound of your voice to remember facts. This actually works very well, and many leaders have used this method when preparing a speech or a presentation. By "calling it out loud" they were to understand the matter at heart and become fluent in the subject matter being spoken.

    d. Physical: The use of Body Movements is where you use the body to express emotions and show activities. It is also where you use the stimuli for the sense of touch.

    e. Oral and Olfactory: The use of smell and taste is an integral part of memory, and many memories are triggered by the smells and tastes, as well as sights and sounds associated with a situation. Using these senses can heighten the effect of a story or message.

3. Emotional display: This principle uses emotions as a method for learning, where emotions are called upon to trigger comprehension to a situation, such as fear of being burnt or crying at the loss of something loved. By setting a specific emotion to real memory, you can enhance the effect of learning through linking emotions to information.

4. Chunking: Breaking or chunking texts into different parts is a simplistic, yet effective, system that works, for instance, breaking up a telephone number into chunks, where the country and city codes are automatic, and the number is all that is needed to be remembered. You learn how to chunk data into core units and link them together, sometimes using memory hooks as an aid.

5. Tell it through a Story: In some instances, when knowledge is hard to explain, telling a story that presents the data is a way to pass it on. This is good for abstract concepts, such as Einstein's theory of the speed of light, where you can deliver complex mathematical concepts alongside graphical imagery to help you remember the core elements of the concept. Tell it through a story uses the multi-sensory approach

and can incorporate one or all of the senses to deliver information.

6. Relaxation. This is where the mind is allowed to rest, gather strength, assimilate information, and be free of overstimulation. It is an integral part of learning; even if you are not actively learning, your mind is still building links and connections, as well as gathering strength when sleeping.

Brain Waves

A word about our brains. The brain has four wavelength patterns:

- Alpha 7-12 Hz
- Beta above 12 Hz
- Delta under 4 Hz
- Theta 4-7 Hz

We will concentrate on two awake levels that are where we will be placed during all AL sessions. These are:

Beta waves, these are the awake wave patterns; when you are awake, you are working at this level.

Alpha waves, these are when you learn the most, and when you reach this level, your learning abilities and brain functions are fully optimized for performance.

Alpha waves can be reached through meditation and other calming techniques that clear the mind and prepare it to focus.

Summing up this chapter

Accelerated Learning is not as complex as it seems, and it is not a rigid system. The give-and-take within the system allows its deployment to take on an amorphous shape. There are vast differences between different schools of thought within the AL community, and some include the use of NLP (Neuro-linguistic Programming) and EQ (emotional intelligence) techniques, which some heckle and others swear by.

In the following chapters, I will present the cores of AL, including all aspects such as timing, frequency, and depth of learning when using AL.

Chunking

George A. Miller introduced the term "chunking" in 1956 when he published his paper "The Magical Number Seven, Plus or Minus Two: Some Limits on our Capacity for Processing Information." Miller presented in his paper the results of research that showed the limitations of memory. His work focused on short-term memory, and his conclusions showed that people retain seven plus or minus two items (5 to 9 items) of information in their short-term storage process of working memory. In contrast, long-term memory stores unlimited amounts of information indefinitely.

This research is important because it shows us that the short-term memory process is our learning bottleneck, where we are limited to a maximum of 9 items, and in some cases, only 5 items of information are being stored at any moment in time. The paper also showed that there is a way to overcome this limitation when you "chunk" data into groups, making the limitations cover more items.

Essentially, Miller suggested we can manage the units of information we collect and look at each unit as a container, which can hold either one or many pieces of information when chunked together. As such, we can magnify our short-term memory process by organizing the data we read, which is termed "chunking."

For example, a unit can be a letter, a word, or even a sentence, a paragraph, a chapter, and a whole story. Now, I do not expect that you can chunk more than a sentence in one go, but if you manage to chunk words, rather than read one at a time, you can improve the short-term memory input and recall long-term memory data much faster.

Take a phone number for the simplest form of chunking; in this case, the number 555-123-4567 can be remembered by chunking the numbers in groups, such as 555, 123, 4567. It would be more efficient and easier to remember in the correct order than trying to input each number separately, such as 5,5,5,1,2,3,4,5,6,7.

Chunking is not just reserved for text or alphanumeric input; it can be for sights, sounds, smells, and all the senses. It is all a matter of organizing the data when inputting for future use.

For example, if you need to organize dates and names, you would best chunk them by date and organize photos under this in a group. This could be useful when needing to remember key dates in history, such as taking the year 1963 and organizing the names of the house of Congress under that date. This would be easier than remembering individual names with a date allocated to each name.

So, we would get 1 chunk of data: 1963; Johnson, Hayden, McCormack.

This is easier than trying to remember 3 chunks of data; Johnson 1963, Hayden 1963, McCormack 1963.

Essentially, what Miller did in 1956 was develop not only the world's first optimized memory retention method, but he also created the world's first true optimized warehouse automation model, which enables warehouse managers to organize items based on an easier and more efficient organizational method. Consider nuts and bolts; you would not store them under individual headings, such as ½" Nut and ¼" Nut, but under the heading Nuts, ½," ¼", where a section is used to store nuts of different sizes and not sizes of different products.

Now, you ask why I referenced warehouse management? Because optimized automated warehouses are perfect examples of how to organize information in the human mind. Think of the mind as a large warehouse, and the "chunking" method is the way we automate incoming data. We need to prepare our minds in a way that will efficiently sort the data before we take it in. This requires preparation, and preparation might sound long and arduous, but it is, in fact, a very easy and simple process that is done instinctively after training.

Intelligent Chunking

Chunking is a process that enables the mind to comprehend larger amounts of data in smaller chunks of collected information; it is essentially the way we create a pattern-based memory system. Chunking is not good for every application; you cannot successfully chunk legal documents since the focus is on detail and understanding every word the way it was placed. The same goes with scientific documents and models.

However, when it comes to storing database style data, it is a perfect method and proven solution.

The types of applications that chunking works with are:

- Grouping vocabulary words by parts of speech
- Grouping Historical events by time periods
- Grouping Countries/Cities by location
- Grouping Artwork or by time periods
- Grouping Musicians by type of music

Recall and Memory Search

One of the by-products of chunking is memory recall, and this improves exponentially when using chunking successfully. You will find that you can recall a lot of data in one chunk using the same process you used to record the data. So, if you want to recall a particular city in the state of Texas, you might find yourself recalling every city you memorized when chunking the cities in the state of Texas.

Chunking Apps

There are a number of chunking apps online for you to try, and they will help train you in the process. Eventually, you will find you are chunking naturally and instinctively. Chunking comes under the memory improvement tools in online apps:

- Brain Trainer for iOS features 10 games for improving your mental capabilities.

- Portrait Health Brain Teasers for iOS is a constantly updated game platform that delivers many mind improvement games.

- Memory Trainer for Android comes with a number of great brain training tools and an interactional task performance tool to improve your performance.

- Brain Workout for Android delivers four core games that help hone your mental capabilities.

- Brainscape for iOS is a unique app that works on improving your cognitive approach and memory and is actually found on education platforms as well as an app.

Ungrouped	Randomly grouped	Rationally grouped		
Beats	Beats			Milk
Bread	Bread	3 Dairy	{	Cream
Butter	Butter			Butter
Carrots				
Cream	Carrots			Parsley
Flour	Cream	4 Produce	{	Carrots
Milk	Flour			Tomatoes
Parsley	Milk			Beats
Pasta				
Tomatoes	Parsley			Bread
	Pasta	3 Starches	{	Pasta
	Tomatoes			Flour

Mind Mapping

Mind maps have been around for centuries, but it was not until the middle of the 20th century when British psychologist Tony Buzan made it a popular tool. Mind mapping is a method that organizes assimilation of information by creating a visual hierarchical representation of the information or in simple terms a map.

Consider a map in its basic form; it is a graphical outlay of a geographical area. You connect cities by roads and show where there are various formations, such as mountains, deserts, rivers, lakes, and coastlines.

Remembering coordinates and how the land appears through a map is the best way to remember the location and navigate. The same can be stated for many other applications, not just geographical use. In fact, maps are used to represent processes and workflow. We use diagrams to show many different processes, and essentially, a mind map is a visual way to remember large amounts of data with details quickly and efficiently.

Mind maps are used to display connections between concepts to help generate ideas and to classify information.

The Mind Map

A mind map is the visual representation of a concept or idea or information in a graphical form and has a basic structure. The structure is used to define levels, connections and build an overall image of a concept in its entirety, with details in each level. So, a good mind map will organize your thoughts, organize the concept, and help you remember and present the information clearly in its entirety and with detail.

A good mind map is made up of a central branch or theme. This is the core of the map, and from this theme, branches emerge that are either linked or singular. Mind maps can show how concepts that seem to be disassociated are actually linked, and the linkage becomes obvious. A good mind mapping technique will eventually teach its user to think in terms of mapping and thus create structural approaches to everyday processes in life.

Mind Mapping Benefits

There are five core benefits from mind mapping, and these include:

- The first is empowering the mind to work comprehensively: Enabling left and right hemispheres of the brain to communicate simultaneously, as the left is analytical, and the right is spatial. When they work together, you create a harmonious balance between the logical left and the creative right.

- The second is teaching you to organize thought and concept.
- The third is to enable you to communicate ideas more efficiently.
- The fourth is to teach you how to find links between seemingly random events.
- The fifth is to teach you how to memorize and remember large amounts of information more efficiently.

The applications for mind mapping are infinite, and in fact, we find maps as a standard of the industry, science, education, and art all around us. Mind mapping is the way we use the saying, "a picture is worth a thousand words." One good mind map will definitely replace a thousand words, if not more.

Buzan's Method

Buzan suggests that, when you want to start a mind map, you follow these steps:

1. Start any new map from the center.

2. Use at least 3 colors and draw the topic's image.

3. Create keywords in print, using either upper or lower-case letters.

4. Always place only one word or an image on every line (node).

5. Lines must start from the central image.

6. Each line starts thick and thins out as it expands outwards.

7. A line must be at least the length of the image or text they support.

8. Use multiple colors, so your eyes are stimulated.

9. Be creative and develop your personal map style.

10. Use emphasized text and images.

11. Show associations, links that are obvious to the eye.

12. Keep a clear map by making the lines outlined within a radial hierarchy.

Mind Map Purpose

Mind maps can be used for just about any subject you think of; they can be used to create a structured process within your mind to help you understand a process or a set of rules. They can also be used to find relations between dissimilar issues that might have a connection, and they can be used to show structures of processes and products.

The concept of using colors is to create a map "key" that will associate the user with a specific issue. For instance, a mind map that has four branches should use four different colors for each branch, and then the branch color will represent all that is on the branch. This organizes the brain to think in terms of categories, and one of the best examples of categorical thinking is in relational database management. Today, most database companies use a mind map structure to define their systems. The main structure or core is called the master data file, and this holds the most important and unchanging information, such as item units of measure, names of suppliers, and material specifications.

This can be applied to the way a mind map is structured, and you learn to create categories through color coding then apply the connecting core or master data from which you then branch out and create all the items, concepts, and processes associated with that central item.

Associations

Essentially, a mind map is a part of a larger mind map, where mind maps link to each other through conceptual nodes. For instance, if we take a mind map of a fish's biology, we will end up with "eyes."These are a shared category with just about every other living animal, and as such, we have at least two central cores to view, fishes and eyes.

In the fish mind map, the eyes are only a branch, but in the eye-mind map, fishes are a branch. Its all a matter of how you view each mind map and its nodes.

Brainstorming

As you can see from associations, a simple mind map is not so simple. It might seem a closed environment, but in fact, most mind maps are all made up of multiple cores, and each core is either a node of one map or a central concept of its own mind map.

Brainstorming allows you to start with a basic concept and, through mind mapping, branch out and find new mind maps and more branches.

Knowing when to stop

As with all infinite systems, and a mind map is an infinite system, you need to know when to stop. Too much information can be detrimental to the mind mapping concept. The issue is to take a basic concept and map it so that you can fully understand its concept and recall it with ease. A good mind map is very spartan but contains enough simple data for you to extrapolate a lot of other information from your mind. As with the fish, we don't need to mind map the entire spectrum of earth genetic system. All we need is to mind map a "trout", so we understand the basics of this animal, where it lives and its living habits, and if you want, how to catch it and cook it.

Mind Mapping Essentials

These are more like tips but will help you when you approach the mind mapping process for the first time.

- Only use keywords or short (two words) phrases; it helps you remember them.
- Draw a box or circle around the keywords or highlight them
- Always draw lines with solid thick starting points, and like real tree branches, thin them out until they reach their end.
- Only write in print; do not make the text hard to read.
- Capitalize main issues; use lower case of secondary.
- Change the size of the text to represent important information and to reinforce the structure.
- Try to use images or icons as much as possible; images are more memorable than words and can represent more words.
- Make sure connections are visible; use extra highlighting, such as thicker lines, or add shapes and frames.
- Without jumbling the page into a jungle, use as many visual cues to emphasize points of value.
- Create a color key for groups, categories, and concepts.

- Use arrows to show connections that are direct, and you can use cross-linkage to show multiple connected nodes. (Try to arrange the nodes, so there is no or little cross-cutting.)
- Mind maps are four-dimensional;this means they represent the 2D images you draw, a 3D spatial for the mind to turn around and view from multiple points, and time, where branches can represent time as well as concepts.
- Important lines can be expressed more boldly.
- Remember, be creative and use your imagination; don't stop your imagination from emerging in even the most absurd sequences. You might be surprised what you will discover.

Finance
Success
Creativity
Tech
Trade
Internet
Cost
Vision
Brand
Control
Time
Money
Ads
Quality
Web Media
Mail
Exposure
Social
Innovation
Analytics
SEO
Goals
Data
Motivation
Sales
Mind Map
Team
Invest
Creativity
Internet
Consumer
Loyalty
Training
People
Management
Vision
Service
Cloud
Device
Retention

Memory Hooks

Memory hooks are a cheap trick into conning your mind to remember something through association. PR and marketing magicians use memory hooks daily to persuade you to buy things you don't need, only because they subconsciously persuaded you that the product is beneficial in some way or another.

Memory hooks use emotions to connect a concept, and these are then given precedence over normal methods of persuasion or studying. The mind links emotion to a concept, and "wham", you have it memorized for life associated with a specific emotion.

Let's look at an example of how a memory hook works in a physical environment. Children learn to fear fire only after they are burnt; this means that, if you tell a child not to play with matches, it will only peak the child's interest, and they will go out of their way to play with matches. However, if the child is given a match to hold when it is lit, they will hold it until the flame reaches their fingers, and then they will drop it because the heat hurt them. This trial by fire is a memory hook. The child now understands that fire hurts.

Now, I don't expect you go cut yourself with a samurai sword to understand how sharp one is, but I do expect you to realize that a memory hook is not just a physical condition. It is also a mental one, and in fact, memory hooks are an adult memory game and not one for children, since they work on your past experiences, using generalized conditions to elicit a response.

For instance, a memory hook can be as vulgar as "this perfume is a skunk." 99% of the world's population has never sought a skunk, much less smelled one, and yet the word Skunk is synonymous with a stench worse than dog shit. Now, notice how you frown when I use the term "dog shit."Why is "skunk" OK but elicits a response of revulsion, and "dog shit" not OK, but elicits the same revulsion? Well, to start, skunk smell comes from a liquid, so we associate a bottle of perfume with a bottle of skunk piss, while dog excrement is solid and is not associated with the liquid perfume.

You see, it's all got to do with society and the way we are brought up. It is also how we associate things, and memory hooks work when you connect the right categories correctly.

Memory hooks are also aptly named, since they trigger memories, and in most cases, bad memories trigger an emotional response far more vividly than a happy memory. It's all got to do with the evolutionary survival instinct.

Now, imagine the "stupid teacher's punishment" (memory hook). I stated stupid teacher and not stupid punishment. The one where you have to write something a hundred times, this is stupid because it does not elicit any emotion other than boredom. This is enough to show you how useless repetitive tasks and cold data reading or writing can be.

In contrast, one simple memory hook can change your life forever.

Visual Memory

Memory hooks work on the visual memory; they elicit an emotional response to something seen or imagined. A good memory hook doesn't need to be too long either; it should be short and concise but strong enough to make you repeat it over and over again by yourself.

You can create a memory hook out of everything and anything. For instance, the Bisaya term Ambot Sa Emo translates to "I don't Know", or "I don't care", depending on which island you are visiting. Now, you want to say I don't care or know but cannot remember the three words, so here goes. The term Ambot Sa Emo sounds like Ambushed Emu, and an ambushed emu sticks its head in the ground;essentially it doesn't know and doesn't care. So, every time I want to say I don't care, I think of an "ambushed emu" sticking its head in the ground and presto…"Ambotsaemo".

Now you can play with this any way you want. As I started out, marketing and PR gurus have been hammering us with memory hooks for years. Let's take a look at a few to get a better picture of what a memory hook looks sounds like.

Memory Hook Examples

Salesmen in the past have used specific words and sentences to elicit a connection. For instance, an IT salesperson might go into an office and look at the wiring and state that you have "fat" wires. He will state, "You have fat wires, you need me"…the word fat is associated with bad, and anything fat is not good, so you need to slim those wires down. A fat wire is a thick one that might be older, using older materials and/or being able to transfer data properly. It really doesn't matter; the fact is that the association of Fat with Wire is visual.

Another memory hook and a derogatory one, when you really listen to it, is, "If you have a face, you need this cream."Obviously, everyone has a face, but when you state it as "if you…" it makes it negative, and the listener immediately thinks, OMG, I have a face…I have a face…:" which obviously they have had since before being born, but now, since they have a face, they will need the cream. Where was that cream before? Who cares?

Now, let's look at some active memory hooks by profession, consider the image you get with the hook.

- Selling footwear: "Walk barefoot with our shoes."
- Plumber: "A flush is better than a full house."
- Electrician: "We check your shorts."
- Lawyer: "When the cops are in the foyer, call Bob, your trusted lawyer."

Memory hooks are a great game, as well as a serious practice to link emotions to information. Just by playing the memory hook game, you start to create new pathways to remembering items and will find yourself practicing memory hooks to help you remember details in everyday life.

Multi-Sensory Learning

Multi-sensory learning (MSL) is a recent science; however, it is based on research that started as far back as the 19th century. Essentially, MSL is a method that promotes the use of more than one sense to learn.

We generally use two senses to learn, sight and sound. In some professions, smell and taste are used too, and others rely on touch. MSL claims learning will improve exponentially when we use at least five senses to remember information, and recall can be triggered by any one or a combination of the senses.

MSL is important for learning since it provides us with more "sensory memory hooks" that we can associate with the subject we want to learn. For instance, when we want to learn how to do geometry, woodwork, biology, and cooking, each subject is multi-sensory, and while you might ask, geometry? The answer is yes. When you study objects, you can look at them, draw them, and feel them. Now, imagine you are given a four-sided pyramid. It is also a triangle and a square. It depends on how you hold it. Now, what if the pyramid is made of stone, wood, or metal? The very touch and feel will help you remember the way a triangle is shaped in three dimensions. Once you start to learn the concept of angles, you will be able to visualize in your mind the sides, shapes, and angles from a visual perspective and not just a mathematical one.

The same goes with using sound and smell; for instance, learning about the life cycle of a cow would require you to sense its living conditions, the smell of nature in winter and summer, the smells of the cow and what is around it. You will also learn a lot when hearing the cow and its movements, as well as even feeling its skin. Using the senses while priming you with data, such as the names of the cow's anatomy, how it eats, what each stomach contains and does, will help you comprehend the cow in its entirety, and when you remember the "cow", you remember it with all the pertinent details you learned to associate with the MSL technique.

Optimized Warehouse

Remember the warehouse I spoke of in the previous methods? Consider this. You have that chunking warehouse where you have grouped your items by a key identifier. Now you have more key identifiers in smell, touch, taste, and sound. You can now categorize information with more accuracy and recall information by using more identifying keys.

MSL Methods

MSL is not about bombarding you with all the senses; it is about associating different senses to heighten the learning process and provide you with a faster learning curve. For instance, when learning a new language, you don't need to smell it or feel it. What you need to do is hear it, so you use sound as the sense to strengthen sight. You read the text, but you should also hear It by vocalizing it aloud. You can also hear it from a video and watch language related movies with English subtitles. Language is about sound; the mind sub-vocalizes it, so help the mind by vocalizing.

MSL styles

Essentially, there are three MSL styles, and these include the visual, auditory, and sensory-motor learners. Each type of person is categorized into one of these groups.

Visual Learners: learn through seeing

You can use diagrams, handouts, illustrations, and maps. These people tend to doodle when listening. It helps them remember what is being stated, and they are aware of your body language and facial expressions. The visual learner is also better at following directions than auditory learners, since they visualize the directions in their mind.

A visual learner will close the eyes to listen and will visualize as they listen. They will benefit from visual methods, such as TV's, PCs, and other digital imaging applications. Most visual learners are usually highly imaginative and are great with a jigsaw and other 3D type puzzles.

Auditory Learners: learn through listening

You can use discussions, lectures, and talking through ideas with auditory learners. They remember all dialogs, jingles, and lyrics with ease and usually talk aloud when concentrating or trying to solve a problem. You might hear them mumble when reading, and they prefer the radio or digital music to visual stimulation. They will be able to follow oral directions with ease and are great phone talkers.

Sensory-motor Learners: learn through moving and touching

You can use tools and appliances, as well as give them hands-on projects to manage, including holding and forming raw materials or assembling. In general, these are fidgeters and don't take well to following instructions. They prefer all things physical, such as sports and engineering, and they prefer active games and making things. They are also comfortable with personal contact.

As you can observe, there are different types of MSL for different people. However, it does not mean you cannot use cross-over methods to improve learning.

Take, for instance, cooking. This is about touch, as well as smell and taste. It is also about being able to follow instructions and to visualize the finished product. A good chef will not shy from touching the liver of a cow or the brain of a sheep and will be at home filleting fishes. At the same time, this chef will understand the nature of heating meat to a specific temperature and not overheating chocolate or sugar, so it doesn't burn, and will listen to the sound of the food boiling, frying, and settling, while looking at the shape and color at each stage of the recipe.

Essentially, a chef is a full MSL person, using every sense to create perfection.

Consider this example and now adapt it for learning a language. You can use music to listen to language, taste food associated with a language and read the text, or watch a movie in a foreign language.

Note Taking

Note taking is essential. It is a very important tool in the AL strategy, and while there is not much to write about note taking, it is necessary to stress the importance of this method.

Note taking is about writing down the words of others or about writing down thoughts. In fact, one of the biggest detrimental issues facing 99% of the population is the fact that they do not write down their thoughts and eventually forget what they had thought.

I am sure you have all thought of something and then on a quick tangent did something else, only getting frustrated at having lost that thought. Well, the solution is simple. Write it down when you think about it. Don't answer the phone, don't answer the call, just write it down, or speak it out to your smartphone to record. With all the latest technologies around, you can easily speak to your cell phone and record all your ideas.

Now, at work, in a meeting, or in college, taking notes is imperative to success. It's not a matter of writing down word for word what you heard. It's about writing down the salient points, in your words, so you remember and understand what is being spoken.

You can also summarize documents, articles, and research; this helps you remember them, as well as help you think up some ideas, which again you need to make a note of.

Also, use mind mapping when note taking. It sometimes helps to create an immediate order out of an initial concept. You create the mind map as the speaker steps through their delivery. The same goes for an idea that you decide to write down.

As you can see, taking notes is not just blindly writing down word for word. It is about being creative in helping your mind remember important information on the go and referring back to this information at a later date.

How to Adapt AL for Everyday Use

Break targets into smaller, achievable milestones

Training your mind to think faster, learn quicker, and remember better is a science. ASL is a system that integrates a number of techniques and methods designed to work together in creating a faster mind learning environment and in helping your mind to operate at a more optimized level.

One of the best ways of implementing ASL is to break down the target into a number of attainable milestones; this will enhance the learning curve by making it gradual and reasonable. For instance, you want to learn a new language.

Don't try to learn the whole language in 6 months in one go. Set some milestones and develop short-term goals that will give you a stepwise progression to your final target that can still be in 6 months.

The best way to look at this is when joining a gym. You don't start lifting heavy weights immediately. You take your time, learning to use each piece of equipment gradually, and then you learn how to integrate nutrition, aerobics, and stretching. You then find yourself setting milestones in terms of sets and weights based on informed understanding, which increases your performance exponentially.

The 80:20 principle of focus

It is considered fact that 20% of all issues make up the most important parts of the issue, while 80% is just filler material. This is the Pareto Principle, and it applied to most subject areas. For instance, 80% of good flavors are made up of 20% of the ingredients found in 80% of the menu items. (Salt is an example.)

The same goes for languages, where 20% of the words are used in 80% of the conversations. This principle states that, when you learn, try to concentrate on the 20% of the important information and do not lose focus on the 80%. Or, as Generals like to state, "concentrate on the main target and forget the collateral issues."

The Pareto principle is all about a lean approach, where you cut out the slack and less useful data in preference for concentrating on what will give you the base for a successful result. However, the big issue with the Pareto principle is that you need to know what that 20% is, and that is the issue with this principle.

Block Distractions

AL is all about focus and concentrates on your goals and targets. Remember the collateral issue with generals? OK, the same goes here. You don't want to be distracted, which means you need to focus on doing one thing perfectly well, rather than ten things not done at all.

Multitasking is OK for a parent. You have to multi-task with children, but when you decide to learn something, don't confuse it by trying to learn two or three some things at the same time. Concentrate on one, get it learned properly, and then move onto the next subject.

Another way of blocking out "white noise" is learning in a controlled environment and focusing on what is important by metering out your workload according to what you need to do on a daily basis.

Practice new skills

Practice makes perfect. Once you have learned something, don't stop practicing it when you decide to start learning something else. For instance, you learned to speak French; don't stop practicing your French now that you have started to learn Microsoft Excel.

One of the biggest mistakes is to stop practicing a newly learned skill and finding out after a while you need to relearn it.

Use mind maps often

As I discussed above, mind maps are amazing tools, and once you get used to creating them, you should use them as often as possible and in all applications. Even at work, a mind map will help you create some interesting insights that others will overlook.

Mind maps are not just used to map out information; they are useful tools to simplify concepts, learn more about the way processes and tasks interlink and evolve.

Break your work into small sessions

Some people find concentrating on work an issue and can burn out easy after a long work period. Therefore, AL teaches us to break down work into 25-minute sessions. Now, this is not a principle you should apply at work. Sometimes, you might need to work for 3-4 hours without stopping, but when learning, it is imperative that you let your brain rest and collate data. Taking short breaks of 5-10 minutes every 25-30 minutes will allow your brain to settle in the information before you continue to input more data.

Test your abilities and knowledge

A popular AL technique is sharing your newly acquired knowledge with a colleague or family member, essentially, learning with their aid in testing your knowledge and advancement. Ask a friend or family member to test you frequently and set yourself goals with KPI's (Key performance indicators). These KPI's are set by you to show how you improve over time.

Relax the Brain

Apart from the 25-30-minute sessions, do not overwork on a daily basis. This means you must set yourself time limits, where you can be with family, friends, and by yourself but without any forced sensory input. Also, take a day off. Weekends are perfect for breaks and important to let your mind and body rest. A reinvigorated mind will always perform better than a tired one.

KPI's for performance control

You already read about KPI's in my piece on family and friend testing. Well, KPI's are more than targets. They are full metrics that can be used to track progress and check your performance. AL is not just about improving the learning experience; it is also about pressuring you into performing better.

Summing up this chapter

Learning is a process, and as with all processes, there are steps to take. It is not a rigid framework, but by following the basics, you will be able to implement every type of AL technique into your daily life. Chunking, Mind Mapping, Memory Hooks and all, each individual technique will work much more efficiently when you practice it with another technique, meshing them into one comprehensive and powerful tool.

Apps and Learning Aids

There are many types of brain improvement apps online. Here is a list of the leading apps that will help you when trying to assimilate AL techniques. Remember, the app is not the technique or the method; it is only an aid that comes to supplement the entire process that begins with intent and motivation.

Lumosity

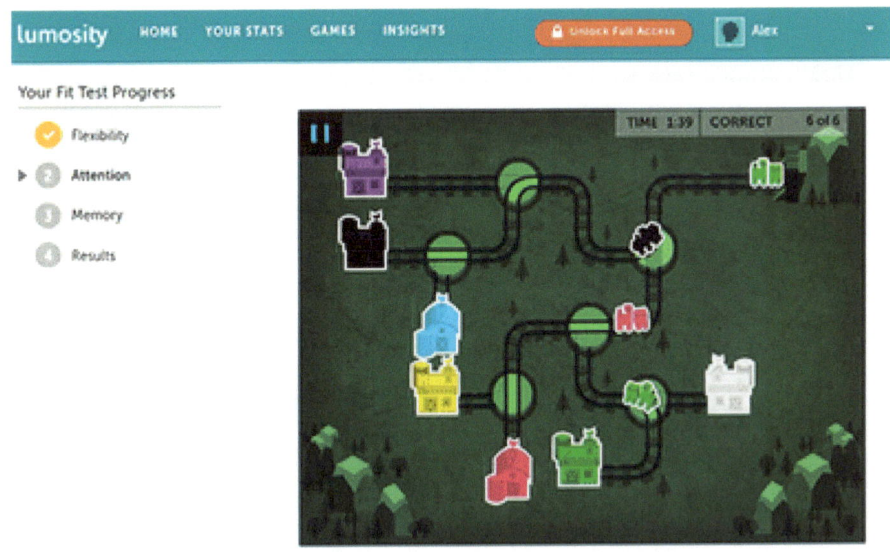

This is a timed app, and it teases your brain with three different games each time. The app focuses on memory, problem-solving, attention span, and thinking. This is considered to be one of the leading brain improvement apps on the circuit.

Fit Brains Trainer

This app delivers 10 sets of games that work on different areas of the brain and aim to improve memory and concentration. You are expected to complete daily tasks and can view your progress on a graph.

CogniFit Brain Fitness

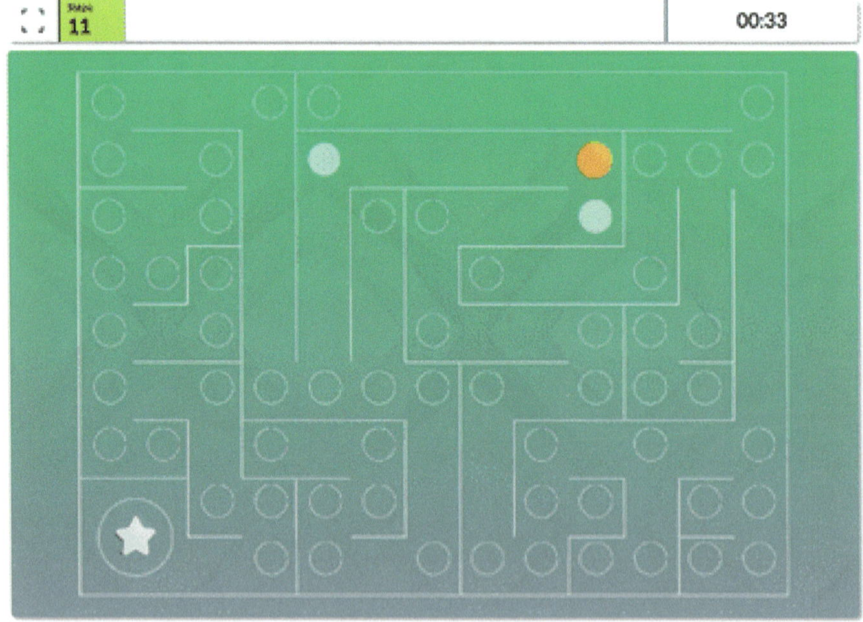

This app was developed by a team that included neuroscientists. You get different levels of play, can track your progress, and is aimed at improving your cognitive thought process. The producers claim that playing this 20 to 30 minutes a day will improve your mind's capabilities.

Brain Fitness Pro

This is an IQ teaser, and I don't take the claim of the makers that it improves your IQ. What I claim is that it will help you improve your logic skills, which can speed up how you handle IQ type questions.

Clockwork Brain

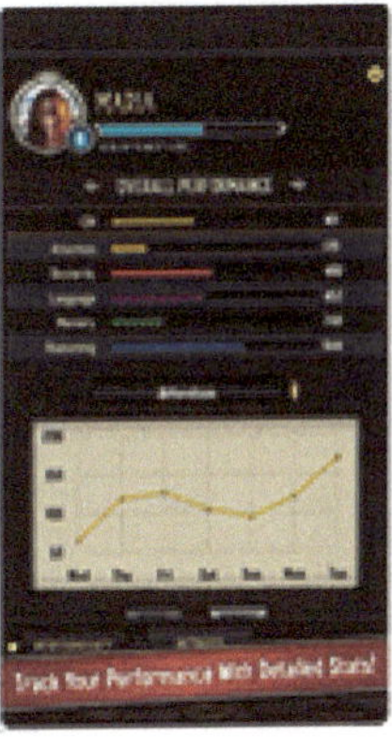

This is a Luminosity type platform with a steampunk environment. Nice games, great graphics, and it helps pass the time by improving your mind.

Eidetic

Eidetic is a memory enhancement app; it is quite an interesting technique that uses 'spaced repetition' to help you memorize information. It is not a chunking method but is well worth the trial to help with memory retention alongside chunking and memory mapping.

Braingle

This is a visual learning tool that riddles your perspective through cleverly crafted graphics. It also helps you learn how to observe without bias, which helps you improve your visual and spatial observational skills.

Not TheHole Story

This is a riddle game that gives you hints and will reveal the result when you give up. Essentially, it is a sort of chunking method that, when used correctly, will test your speed reading skills and see if you maintain an eye for detail.

Personal Zen

This is a relaxant, based on a visual meditation model. Here, you follow the journey of two animated characters traveling through a field of grass. The advice of this apps developer is that you use this once a day for 10minutes to reduce anxiety. This is a good tool for preparing your mind before starting a studying session or for breaking the monotony in a laborious session.

Conclusion

This book presented you with a number of key elements that make up the accelerated learning method. AL is constantly evolving, and as we learn more about the brain and how it functions, so too do we continue to improve learning methodologies to improve knowledge assimilation.

However, no matter how ingenious we become, it is the individual that has to take the first step to gain more knowledge more efficiently, and this requires a number of personal dedications, which are:

Preparing to Learn

Learning is simple. All you need to do is be prepared to learn, and this requires dedication to results. There is no point in starting to learn if you don't intend to follow through the whole process or if you will learn and then forget. Preparing to learn is about preparing the mind and preparing yourself for what you will do with the knowledge you gain.

There are a few steps to take before starting a new subject, and these include an overview of the subject. What does it include, how many hours will you need to apply every day to succeed, and what will be the end product of all the studies?

These questions lead you to the next step, which is:

Motivation

Motivation is what drives you to succeed, and when you start to learn a new subject, the motivation has to be something that starts at the core of your desire. High motivation would include learning to improve your professional status or teaching you a new profession to complement or replace your current one. Motivation can be from the necessity to improve a commercial application, such as learning Chinese to negotiate with Chinese businesses, or for love, such as learning how to paint or sculpt.

Once you convert the reason you want to learn into a core motivated function, then you will find that you will learn much faster and with more vigor.

Whole Brain

As I mentioned in this book, the left and right hemispheres of the brain process in different modes. The left is analytical, and the right is creative. This means that the left will do all the math's and logic, while the right will do all the imagining and artistry. The left is conceptual; the right is spatial. Essentially, when an individual is oriented to a particular subject, you can see which hemisphere that person's brain works with. Lawyers, Physicist, and Accountants work with their left hemisphere, while dancers, artists and web designers work with their right. Some professions work with both, such as physicians and architects.

Now add to this the limbic system, which manages our long-term memory. The limbic system decides what it will remember based on emotional content, and this is why memory hooks are so successful and why MSL is so important.

Summing Up

I hoped you enjoyed this book, and use its content to improve your learning capabilities. You will find that learning can be more fun than playing games, and in fact, information gathering, process understanding, and conceptualizing is an exciting real-time and real-life activity that helps you improve while enjoying the benefits of increasing your knowledge and understanding.

If you enjoyed this book or received value from it in any way, then I'd like to ask you for a favor: would you be kind enough to leave a review for this book on Amazon? It'd be greatly appreciated!

https://www.amazon.com/dp/B07H442QDD/

If you want to be aware of Alex Medler's new book releases, giveaways & special offers please click the link below

http://dexlerbooks.com/alex-medler